MW00959367

iPhone for Seniors

A Beginner's Comprehensive Step-by-Step User Guide

Elbert Walker

CONTENT

Introduction

Welcome to **"iPhone for Seniors,"** your one-stop shop for explaining the sometimes confusing world of iPhone use. You've come to the correct place if you've ever picked up an iPhone and wondered what the big deal was about, or if you've ever been confused by a bewildering assortment of vibrant icons and unfamiliar lingo.

Knowing how to use your iPhone well is more crucial than ever in a time when digital expertise is nearly as valuable as the cash in your wallet. It serves as a tool for entertainment, a camera to record moments, a communication tool, and much more. However, let's face it: all of this functionality may appear intimidating to beginners.

You are the reason behind the "iPhone for Seniors" design. Our goal is to simplify the complexities of using an iPhone into manageable, clear sections. We can assist you with making simple phone calls, sending emoji-filled texts to pals, taking the ideal picture, or browsing the enormous selection of apps on the App Store.

- **Advanced capabilities:** Explore settings that let you tailor your iPhone to your own requirements, such as battery optimization methods and accessibility capabilities.

- **Security and Privacy:** In this day and age, where data is valuable, we'll walk you through putting up security measures to safeguard your information.

- **Maintaining Touch:** We'll look at several strategies to stay in touch with your loved ones wherever they may be, including social media, video calls, and instant messaging apps.

- **Your iPhone** is more than just a tool for communication; it's also a health companion. Acquire the skills to track your sleep, your steps, and even to remind yourself to drink enough water.

- **Amusement:** Ways to Have Fun with Your iPhone! We'll show you how to amuse yourself with your smartphone by playing games, streaming your favorite movies, and listening to   podcasts.

With simple-to-follow videos, hints, and techniques that even seasoned iPhone users will find helpful, we'll walk you through each topic. It can be difficult to stay up to date with the rapid advancements in technology. To make sure you stay on top of things, we'll update this series often.

That means that **"iPhone for Seniors"** has something to offer everyone, regardless of whether you've just opened your first iPhone or have been using one for a while and want to improve. Come along as we break down the amazing possibilities, capabilities, and functionalities that come with owning an iPhone. Right at your fingertips, a world of exploration awaits you.

Chapter 1: Getting Started with Your iPhone

Greetings from your new iPhone's wonderful world! We'll walk you through the first steps of configuring your device, familiarizing yourself with its physical attributes, and connecting to necessary networks in this chapter. This chapter will make sure you're ready to go on your iPhone journey, whether you're unwrapping your device for the first time or just want to brush up on some basics.

Take Out Your iPhone

It's a unique experience to unbox your iPhone. When the gadget is carefully taken out of its package, you'll be holding a sophisticated and effective instrument in your hands. Pause to admire the creativity and skill that went into making this gadget before you turn it on.

Turning on and setting up initially

Holding down the Side button, which is usually found on the right side of the phone, will turn on your iPhone by displaying the Apple logo. Select your Wi-Fi network, language, and region by following the on-screen directions. Never be afraid to seek for help if you have any questions about any step.

Comprehending Controls and Buttons

To interact with your iPhone, there are a number of physical buttons and controls on it:

- Side Button: This button can be used to snap screenshots, turn on or off Siri, and operate your iPhone in many other ways.

- The volume of your calls, media playing, and notifications are all controlled by these buttons.

- Ring/Silent Switch: This switch alternates between vibrating or not making any sound in the ring mode (sound on).

- Home Button (on earlier models): When using an older iPhone model, you can enter multitasking and go back to the Home Screen by pressing this button.

Making a connection to cellular and Wi-Fi networks

Making a Wi-Fi connection is a vital step in configuring your iPhone. Compared to cellular data, an internet connection over a Wi-Fi network is quicker and more reliable. Choose your network from the list under Settings > Wi-Fi to establish a connection. Provide a correct password if prompted to do so.

Your iPhone can also access the internet via mobile data if you have a cellular plan. But be aware that using your mobile data for extensive online browsing could result in extra fees. Go to Settings > Cellular to activate or deactivate cellular data.

Configuring Touch ID (on models that support it) or Face ID

The sophisticated biometric authentication techniques found on modern iPhones, such as Face ID and Touch ID, offer a safe and practical way to unlock your phone, make purchases, and access apps. To set up Touch ID (which uses your fingerprint) or Face ID (which uses face recognition) during initial setup or later in Settings, follow the on-screen instructions.

Finishing Up the First Setup

Options to restore from an iTunes or iCloud backup and to set up as a fresh device will appear as you move through the setup process. Select the option most appropriate to your circumstances. To ensure a fresh start for your iPhone experience, set it up as a new device if you're new to it.

1.1 Why This Book is for You

As a senior trying to get the most out of your iPhone, we'll get into the reasons why this book is exactly what you need in this chapter. While adopting new technology can be a little intimidating, don't worry—this book is meant to make the process of learning easy, fun, and empowered.

Using Current Technology

If you haven't used a smartphone in a while, you may be asking why knowing about the iPhone is important to you. Actually, there are a ton of opportunities that the iPhone presents to you that can improve your life in a variety of ways.

Human connection is fundamentally based on communication, and the iPhone has made it simpler than ever to keep in touch with loved ones. The iPhone helps people connect across generations and geographical boundaries, whether it's through video calls with your grandchildren, short texts to friends, or sharing images with relatives across the nation.

Getting Around with Confidence

Gaining more self-assurance when using the iPhone is one of the book's primary goals. You're not alone in this journey, even though we recognize that technology can occasionally feel daunting. We will walk you through each idea step-by-step so that you understand it before going on to the next. By the time you've finished reading this book, you'll be confidently swiping, tapping, and exploring your iPhone.

Eliminating Technology's Fear

Especially if you're not used to smartphones or touchscreens, it's fair to be wary about utilizing new technology. But the iPhone is a great option for seniors because of its simple design and easy-to-use interface.

Specifically Made for You

This book is written especially for seniors, with your own needs and preferences in mind. We have created explanations and directions that are easy to comprehend, brief, and straightforward because we recognize that your demands may be different from younger users'.

Opening Up New Adventures

The iPhone is a means of exploring new things as well as a communication tool. The iPhone can improve your life in unexpected ways, from using it to explore the enormous world of the internet to finding new books, music, and apps. Opening doors to study, creativity, and pleasure is more important than merely utilizing technology.

Starting the Adventure

Remember that learning is a process that happens gradually as you work your way through the chapters in this book. You can use your iPhone confidently and independently with each concept you understand. Hence, this book is your guide to maximizing the potential of your iPhone, regardless of your level of experience with technology.

In the upcoming chapters, we'll begin by going over the fundamentals of your iPhone, walking you through its key features and assisting you in laying a strong foundation. Keep in mind that we are here to support you at every stage of your trip. This is your adventure.

1.2 Navigating the iPhone Interface

Welcome to the world of the UI on your iPhone! This chapter will take you on a journey to comprehend the basic components of the layout and style of your gadget. Seniors like you will find the iPhone's UI to be entertaining and approachable because to its design, which prioritizes simplicity and ease of use.

Your Digital Hub, the Home Screen

The bright and well-organized Home Screen, which houses all of your apps and features, greets you when you activate your iPhone. Every icon stands for an app, which is a portal to endless possibilities. Your Home Screen is your portal to everything, from chat to photos, entertainment to planning.

Folders and App Icons

The Home Screen has your apps organized in tidy rows and columns. Any application icon can be tapped to open that particular application. You may swipe left and right to access further screens that house even more apps, so don't panic if you can't find one straight away.

Additionally, you may folder-organize your programs. Just tap and hold an app icon until it begins to wiggle to accomplish this. Next, to create a folder, drag one program over another. Within the folder, you can add relevant programs and give it a name. For example, to organize all of your game apps in one location, you may establish a "Games" folder.

The Dock: Easy Way to Access Your Favorites

The Dock, a dedicated section that offers rapid access to your most frequently used apps, is located at the bottom of the Home Screen. This implies that your preferred programs are right here, easily accessible, saving you the trouble of searching through several screens.

The apps you use most frequently can be added to the Dock by customizing it. You just need to tap and hold the app icon and drag it to the Dock in order to add it. You can delete an app by holding down the icon in the Dock and choosing "Remove from Dock."

How to Navigate Within Apps

An app's interface and functionalities are exclusive to it once you open it. Gestures like pinching, swiping, and tapping are frequently used for app navigation. A few typical gestures are as follows:

- Tap: Tapping on a button or symbol typically causes an action to be carried out, like playing a song or opening an email.

- Swipe: To move within apps or to scroll through lists, pages, or images, swipe left, right, up, or down.

- Pinch: You can zoom in or out by spreading your fingers apart and pinching together when you place two fingers on the screen.

- These movements are meant to be simple to use and intuitive, so don't be scared to experiment with them.

How to Use the Control Center

The Control Center, a quick-access menu to important settings like Wi-Fi, Bluetooth, brightness, and more, can be accessed by swiping down from the top-right corner of the screen. This adds even more convenience to using your iPhone by removing the need to search through settings menus.

Your Panel, Your Style

Always keep in mind that the iPhone's UI is designed to be customizable to your preferences. You may modify your device's wallpaper, reorganize its apps, and add personal touches to make it uniquely you. You are here because the iPhone is here to help, and this chapter is just the start of your path to become an expert user of its interface.

We'll go deeper into the core functions of your iPhone in the upcoming chapter, covering everything from sending and receiving messages to staying in touch. Prepare to explore these key features and gain even more familiarity with the iPhone's interface.

1.3 Understanding Buttons and Controls

Welcome to the chapter where you will learn about the controls and physical features of your iPhone. We'll walk you through the buttons and other components that let you interact with your smartphone in this chapter, so you can learn about their uses and purposes. To navigate your iPhone confidently and easily, it's essential to understand these buttons and features.

Your Command Center is the Side Button.

With the exception of the iPhone SE 2nd generation and iPhone 12 models, which are located on the right side of the device, the Side button operates as a flexible command center for a number of purposes.

- Turn On/Off: To turn on or off your iPhone, press and hold the Side button. When you first unboxed your iPhone, you used this exact button to turn it on.
- Siri: To use Apple's speech assistant, simply press and hold the Side button. Using voice commands, you can send messages, make reminders, ask Siri questions, and accomplish a lot more.
- Emergency SOS: This feature, which contacts emergency services and shares your position with pre-designated contacts, can be activated by quickly pressing the Side button five times in a row.
- Take a screenshot by simultaneously pressing the Side and Volume Up buttons to record what's currently on your screen.

Investigating Your New iPhone

You can now explore the features, apps, and potential of your iPhone after completing the initial setup. Your iPhone is a multipurpose tool that can improve your life in many ways. It can be used for messages, calls, web surfing, and photo taking.

Mastery of Audio: Volume Buttons

There are two volume keys on the left side of your iPhone: Volume Down (-) and Volume Up (+).

Control Notifications with the Ring/Silent Switch

The Ring/Silent switch, which is situated directly above the Volume controls, lets you switch between ring and silent mode quickly:

- Your iPhone will make noises for calls, messages, and notifications when it is in Ring Mode, which is indicated by the switch facing the screen and not showing orange.

- You can set your iPhone to vibrate or remain silent for incoming calls and notifications when the switch is in the "Silent" position (orange).

Central Navigation is the Home Button on older versions.

The Home button serves as a primary navigation function on iPhones with a physical button (such the iPhone 8 and previous models):

- Return to Home Screen: From any app or screen, press the Home button once to get back to the Home Screen.
- To utilize multitasking, double-press the Home button to bring up the App Switcher. This will show you your most frequently used apps so you can navigate quickly.

1.4 Connecting to Wi-Fi and Cellular Networks

Welcome to the chapter that explains the wonders of maintaining connections in the modern world. This chapter will walk you through setting up Wi-Fi and cellular networks on your iPhone. These connections are your device's lifelines since they let you browse the web, talk to loved ones, and access a multitude of educational and entertainment resources.

The Strength of WiFi

Your iPhone and the internet are connected via Wi-Fi, which functions as a virtual freeway. Your device uses the internet that is supplied by a wireless router when it is linked to Wi-Fi; these routers are usually found in homes, offices, or public spaces like coffee shops and libraries. Using WiFi is as follows:

- To gain access to Settings, use the iPhone's Settings app.

- Menu for Wi-Fi: Press "Wi-Fi," which is typically the first item on the list.

- Wi-Fi networks that are currently available will be listed. To establish a connection, tap on the network name.

- In the event that the network is secured, you will be required to input the Wi-Fi password. If you type it correctly, your iPhone will connect.

- Connected: When the connection is established, a checkmark will appear next to the network name to show that you are online.

Accepting Data from Cells

Your iPhone can use cellular data to access the internet when you're not near Wi-Fi networks. Cellular data is a terrific way to stay connected when Wi-Fi is unavailable, but it is dependent on the network of your carrier. Remember that if you use a lot of data, your cellular plan may charge you more. Here's how to turn on or off cellular data:

- To gain access to Settings, use the iPhone's Settings app.

- Scroll down and select "Cellular" or "Mobile Data" from the Cellular Menu, according on your location.
- Cellular Data Toggle: Toggle the feature on or off by tapping the toggle next to "Cellular Data".

Wireless Assistance: Smooth Transitions

One useful feature on your iPhone is called Wi-Fi Assist. When turned on, it makes sure that when your Wi-Fi connection wanes, your internet experience remains steady by seamlessly switching between Wi-Fi and cellular data. To switch Wi-Fi Assist on or off:

- To gain access to Settings, use the iPhone's Settings app.

- Cellular Menu: Select "Cellular" or "Mobile Data" by swiping down.

- Swipe down to turn on or off "Wi-Fi Assist."

Everything You Need at One Place

Once your iPhone is linked to Wi-Fi or cellular connection, you may begin exploring the virtual environment. These connections provide you limitless options for everything from messaging to web browsing to streaming videos to using apps. The capacity to connect is a key to knowledge, communication, and amusement, whether you're researching subjects you're interested in or keeping in touch with loved ones.

The features that make use of these connections—such as messaging, online browsing, and accessing necessary apps—will be covered in more detail in the next chapters. So, as you continue using your iPhone, prepare ready to enjoy the potential of keeping connected.

Chapter 2: Making and Receiving Calls

Here you have arrived at the center of iPhone communication. This chapter will walk you through the basic, yet crucial, procedure of placing and taking calls. Your iPhone is more than just a gadget; it's a means of communication with your friends, family, and coworkers. Knowing how to make and take calls is essential to making the most out of your mobile, whether you're interacting with loved ones or organizing with friends.

Making a Contact

On your iPhone, placing a call is as simple as tapping a button. To do this, follow these steps:

- To use the Phone app, find and tap the green symbol on your home screen.

- Dialing Numbers: To make a call, enter the desired number on the keypad. You can start entering the name and suggestions will come up if the number is saved in your Contacts.

- Call Button: To start a call after entering a number, hit the green Call button.

- Call in Progress: You can mute, put the call on speaker, and add another call while it's in progress.

Getting a Call

Your iPhone notifies you of incoming calls through a ringing sound and a notification on the screen. Here's how you take a phone call:

- Incoming Call Notification: When a call comes in, your iPhone shows you the number or, if it's not in your Contacts, the caller's name.

- Answering: Slide the green "Answer" button to the right to take a call. The caller will be connected to you as a result.

- Sliding the red "Decline" button to the left indicates that you do not wish to answer the call. In addition, you can turn off the ringing by using the Side or Volume Up/Down buttons.

Unanswered Calls and Voicemail

A caller can leave a voicemail on your iPhone if you are unavailable to answer it. Your iPhone notifies you when a call is missed and shows the number of missed calls as a badge on the icon of the Phone app.

- Voicemail Check: Your iPhone will notify you if you have a voicemail. To view and hear your voicemails, tap "Voicemail" on the Phone app.

- Returning Calls: To retrieve your call history, open the Phone app, select the "Recents" option, and then dial the number you missed. To make a call back, tap on the missed call entry.

Call Configurations and Features

In order to improve your calling experience, the iPhone offers the following call-related options and features:

- Favorites: To facilitate fast access, add contacts you call frequently to your Favorites list. on order to manage this list, tap "Favorites" on the Phone app.

- Caller ID: Select if you want your phone number to show up on the other end of the call. For further information, go to Settings > Phone > Show My Caller ID.

- Make video calls with other Apple users by utilizing the FaceTime application. Even if they live far away, it's a terrific opportunity to visit and speak with loved ones in person.

2.1 Dialing Numbers

This is the chapter where you will learn how to dial numbers on your iPhone. We'll walk you through using the keyboard efficiently, storing contacts, and making phone calls in this chapter. Dialing numbers is a basic ability that opens doors to important conversations and interactions, whether you're reaching out to family, friends, or services.

The Keypad's Use

You can immediately dial phone numbers using the iPhone's keypad. It has a straightforward, user-friendly design that looks like a conventional phone keypad. Using it is as follows:

- Phone App Access: Click on the Phone app from your home screen.

- Keypad Tab: Select the "Keypad" tab located at the bottom of the screen within the Phone app.

- Dialing Numbers: To make a phone call, enter the desired number on the keyboard. Press the corresponding number buttons on the phone number.

- Clear and Delete: To remove the final digit you entered incorrectly, hit the "Delete" button, which is symbolized by a backspace arrow. Slide the "Clear" button (sometimes marked "C" or "AC") to clear the entire number.

- Dial Button: To start a call after entering the number accurately, hit the green "Call" button.

Making International Calls

The country code must be entered when calling an international number. The country-specific international access code is substituted with the "+" symbol. Here's how to call a number from overseas:

- Launch the Phone app in order to access it.

- Select the "Keypad" tab by tapping on it.

- To input "+," tap and hold the "0" button until the sign "+" shows up.

- Dial Country Code: Input the destination nation's country code.

- Enter Phone Number: Proceed to enter the remaining phone number as normal, following the country code.

- Dial Button: Press the green "Call" button to start a conversation.

Contacts Are Saved

The Contacts app on your iPhone allows you to save contacts, which makes phoning even more convenient. In this manner, whenever you wish to make a call, you won't have to manually dial or recall numbers. To save a contact, follow these steps:

- Contacts App Access: From your Home Screen, launch the Contacts app.

- Create a new contact by tapping the "+" or "Add" button.

- Details to be entered include the contact's name, phone number, and any other data you wish to store.

- To save the contact, either tap "Done" or "Save".

Getting in Contacts to Make Calls

Contacts that you have stored are simple to locate and contact on your iPhone:

- Launch the Phone app in order to access it.

- Tap the "Contacts" tab located at the bottom of the screen.

- Locate Contact: To locate the person you wish to call, either browse through your contacts or use the search bar.

- Call Contact: Tap the name of the contact to see their details, then tap the number that you wish to call.

- Dial Button: Press the green "Call" button to start a conversation.

A Communication Opening

You can connect with the world around you by having the fundamental abilities of dialing numbers and storing contacts. The contacts and keypad on your iPhone facilitate easy communication, whether you're reaching out to services, scheduling an appointment, or placing a call to a buddy.

We'll explore apps, talk more about messaging, and find other methods to use your iPhone for communication in the next chapters. Prepare to increase your connectedness and take advantage of everything that technology has to offer.

2.2 Answering and Ending Calls

Finishing a Call

It is as easy to end a call as it is to begin one. When it's time to hang up, follow these steps to stop the call:

- During the Call: An interface showing the speaker selections, call duration, and other information will appear to you when on a call.

- Button to End Call: Tap the red "End Call" button to end the call. Usually, this button takes the place of the green "Call" button that you pressed to answer the call.

- Speaker and silence Options: You can utilize these features to access the dial pad, turn on speakerphone, or silence the call while it's in progress.

- Turning Down Phone Calls and Sending a Message

2.3 Managing Contacts

Making New Relationships

You can make sure you have all the information you need at your fingertips by following the simple steps to add new contacts to your iPhone. To make a new contact, follow these steps:

- Contacts App Access: From your Home Screen, launch the Contacts app.

- To add a contact, simply tap the "+" or "Add" button, which is often found in the upper-right corner of the screen.

- Details to be entered include the contact's name, contact number, email address, and any other details you choose to keep on file, including home address or job details.

- To save the contact in your address book, tap either "Done" or "Save".

Modifying Connections

Every now and then, contacts update their addresses, phone numbers, and other information. You can edit contacts that are already in your address book to keep it current. To do this, follow these steps:

- Open the Contacts app in order to access it.

- Choose Contact to find the contact you wish to modify by either scrolling through your contacts or using the search bar.

- Edit Contact: Tap the name of the contact to see their information. Next, click "Edit" located in the upper-right corner of the screen.

- Modify: Make any necessary updates to the contact's details, such as adding a new phone number or email address.

- Save: To save the modifications you've made, tap "Done".

Getting in Touch

When you need to get in touch, being organized with your contacts will help you locate the proper person fast. Here are some pointers to help you arrange your contacts:

- Favorites: List people you communicate with often as favorites for easy access. You can add someone to your Favorites list by tapping the star icon next to their name.

- Groups: To organize your contacts and make it simpler to send emails or messages to particular groups of people, create custom contact groups.

- Sorting: Typically, contacts are arranged alphabetically by first name. This can be adjusted to order by last name under Settings > Contacts > order Order.

- Search: To quickly locate a particular contact by name, use the search box at the top of the Contacts app.

iCloud Sync and Backups

Your iCloud account will automatically backup your iPhone's contacts, ensuring that your data is safe and recoverable in case of emergency. All of your Apple devices may access your contacts thanks to iCloud sync. iCloud sync can be enabled in Settings > [your name] > iCloud > Contacts.

Strengthening Bonds

Keeping your relationships with friends, family, and coworkers strong is the goal of contact management, which goes beyond simple information organization. You can converse more effectively and maintain easy contact if your address book is kept up to date.

We'll delve into important apps that can improve your iPhone experience in the next chapters, as well as other communication options like video calls and messaging. Your ability to cultivate relationships and confidently traverse the digital world will improve as you handle your contacts with style.

Chapter 3: Texting and Messaging

This chapter introduces you to the world of texting and messaging on your iPhone. Your iPhone provides a variety of messaging alternatives to help you stay in touch with friends, family, and coworkers in this digital age where communication has transcended traditional phone calls.

Text Message (SMS) Sending

Short Message Service (SMS) text messages are a rapid and effective form of communication. How to send a text message is as follows:

- New Message Start: To begin a new message, tap the pencil icon, which is often found in the upper-right corner.

- Recipient: Type the recipient's phone number or name in the "To:" space. To select a contact from your address book, you can also hit the "+" symbol.

- Write Message: To begin writing your message, tap the text field located at the bottom of the screen.

Transmitting MMS (Multimedia Messages)

You can attach images, videos, audio samples, and more to your text messages with multimedia messages (MMS). To send an MMS, follow these steps:

- Open the Messages app to gain access to it.

- Create a New Message: Press the pencil symbol to begin a new communication.

- receiver: Type in the name or phone number of the receiver.

- hit the camera icon to shoot a picture or a video, or hit the "+" icon to select media from your device's gallery, to add media.

- Write Message: You can optionally include a text message.

- To send a multimedia message, simply tap the blue "Send" button.

How to Use iMessage for Improved Messaging

Apple's in-house texting service, iMessage, offers advanced functionalities like typing indicators, read receipts, and more. When utilizing Apple devices, both the recipient and you can access it. Blue bubbles represent messages sent using iMessage. Using iMessage is explained here:

- Open the Messages app to gain access to it.

- Create a New Message: Press the pencil symbol to begin a new communication.

  receiver: Type in the name or phone number of the receiver

- Type your message in the text field to compose it.

- Transmit an iMessage: When the message bubble goes blue, iMessage is accessible. To send an iMessage, tap the blue "Send" button.

Investigating Messaging Apps

There are more messaging apps with special capabilities for communication than SMS and iMessage:

- WhatsApp: A well-known messaging program that allows texting, online video calls, and phone conversations. End-to-end encryption is provided, and it is cross-platform.

- Facebook Messenger: Communicate via text, voice calls, and video calls with pals on Facebook. Messenger can be used without a Facebook account as well.

- Telegram: An online messaging service featuring self-destructing messages and hidden chats, Telegram is well-known for its security features and group chat functionality.

- Signal: A messaging app with a privacy focus that prioritizes data protection and robust encryption. Because of its dedication to user privacy, it is well appreciated.

Taking Up Contemporary Communications

Modern communication revolves around texting and messaging. They let you communicate with friends and family in real time about your ideas, feelings, and emotions. You're opening up a world of instant connection and communication as you become an expert text and multimedia message sender.

3.1 Sending and Receiving Text Messages

The Discussion Canvas

With each tap of your fingertips, text messages turn your iPhone into a conversational canvas that helps you and the person you're texting bridge the gap between you. Texting encapsulates the essence of the moment and transfers it into the digital sphere, whether you're checking in, sharing great news, or expressing appreciation.

Formulating Your Reply

Texting is like writing a little artwork. Here's how to write a message that really gets through:

- Personalization: To establish a feeling of closeness and connection right away, address the receiver by name.

- Clarity: Clearly and succinctly state your ideas. Keep messages short; else, they could lose their impact.

- Emotion: Use emoticons, GIFs, or language that expresses your feelings to add emotion to your communication.

- Context: Give your message some background information if necessary, particularly if you think the receiver may not be familiar with the topic.

Excitement and Immediate Reward

The instantaneous nature of text texts is their enchantment. Upon clicking "Send," your message appears on the recipient's smartphone immediately. You can feel the tension rising with each type indication tick—the sender waiting for a response, and the recipient composing their answer.

Getting a Reaction

An emotional symphony begins the instant a response is received. The reaction is a virtual embrace that reassures you of your connection, whether it's a torrent of words, a single emoji, or even simply a thumbs-up. It serves as a reminder that you are a part of this digital dance, that your words matter, and that you are not alone in this conversation.

Time and Courtesies

Though text messaging allows for spontaneity, it's important to remember basic manners to ensure that your conversations run smoothly:

- Response Time: Respecting the conversation is demonstrated by prompt responses. People understand that life gets busy, so don't worry about getting an answer right away.

- Reading the Room: Take note of the conversation's tenor and modify your answers accordingly. More careful thought may be needed when discussing sensitive subjects.

Accepting the Adventure

Texting someone is like taking a trip through a story that reveals itself one character at a time. It's a patchwork of ideas, feelings, and relationships that mimics how we speak to each other in the contemporary world. Regardless of the physical distance that separates individuals, texting is a dance of communication that pulls people closer together—from the soothing chime of a new message to the satisfaction of a meaningful reply.

We will continue to delve into the various ways your iPhone can be used for communication in the next chapters, covering everything from video chats to phone conversations. Remember that every message you send and receive adds to the exquisite story of the connections in your life as you participate in the dance of digital words.

3.2 Using iMessage and Emojis

The Language of Symbols: Emojis

Emojis have evolved from being simple images to a universal language that cuts across linguistic and cultural barriers. Even complex ideas and feelings that could take volumes to explain in language can be expressed with just one emoji. Using emojis to your advantage is as follows:

- To access the emoji keyboard, tap the smiley face symbol next to the text field when you're typing a message.

- Peruse and Look for: Peruse the many emoji categories or utilize the search bar to locate particular emojis based on their name or keyword.

- Emojis are a great way to express your feelings, from happiness ☐ to laughter ☐ to sadness ☐ , and all the emotions in between.

- Improve Messages: Emojis can be used to emphasize points, add humor, or improve the overall tone of writing.

- Make Stories: Emojis can be used to make brief stories or visual humor. Build stories that connect with your receiver by letting your imagination go wild.

Taking Pleasure in Play and Nuance

Emojis' capacity to bring subtlety and humor to your talks is what makes them so beautiful. An emoji can transform a straightforward "Okay" into a cordial consent □□. It can express joy □, affection □, or even a hint of irony □. The emotions that permeate your speech can be painted on an emoji canvas.

How to Use Emojis Skillfully

Emojis make your messages more endearing, but there are a few things to keep in mind while using them:

- Context Matters: To prevent misunderstandings, use emojis that are appropriate for the conversation's context.

- Avoid Overusing Emojis: Although emojis can improve your messages, using too many of them can lessen their impact.

- Cultural Sensitivity: Recognize that emojis can mean different things in different cultures.

Beyond Words Expression

Emojis and iMessage combine to provide an expressive symphony that is unmatched by words. Your iPhone becomes a canvas for creativity and connection, from endearing dialogues to humorous banter. As you delve into iMessage and the wide universe of emojis, keep in mind that every message is a chance to express your feelings and ideas in vivid detail and make a lasting mark on your online exchanges.

We'll keep exploring the different ways your iPhone may communicate, from voicemails to video conversations, in the next chapters. As you get proficient with iMessage and emoticons, you're learning about the expressive and lighthearted aspect of communication that goes well with verbal language.

3.3 Managing Conversations

Here's the chapter where we explore the fine art of using your iPhone to manage conversations. Finding the ideal balance between being connected and preserving your peace of mind is crucial in a world where messages, alerts, and updates are everywhere. We'll look at conversation management techniques in this chapter to make sure your iPhone improves your connections without becoming too much.

The Digital Storm

With smartphones, discussions can now come from anywhere in your life. It's simple to get sucked into a digital torrent of emails, texts, and social media updates. Having healthy relationships while preserving your mental space is the goal of conversation management, not just sifting through communications.

Putting Communication First

Prioritizing is the first step in conversation management. Not every communication needs to be answered right away, and not every notification from an app needs to be opened. Effective communication can be prioritized in the following ways:

- Favorites: Add your closest contacts to your favorites list so that their messages will always be visible, even when your phone is mute.

- Notifications: Set up each app's notification preferences. Give high-priority apps permission to get notifications; for less important apps, think about reducing or suppressing them.

Putting Talks in Orde

Maintaining an orderly list of conversations aids in keeping track of your exchanges. Here's how to maintain the orderliness of your conversations:

- Group Chats: If you participate in more than one group chat, think about muting the ones that aren't really necessary. You won't receive a barrage of notifications in this manner.

- Archiving: Keep track of discussions that aren't ongoing now but might be later on. This clears out the clutter from your primary chat list without erasing important correspondence.

Reacting Intentionally

Your talks will be more relevant and interesting if you respond carefully:

- Quality Over Quantity: Sent thoughtful replies are preferable to hurried ones sent merely for the sake of replying.

- Provide Context: If it's necessary, especially if the conversation has advanced, provide context when answering after a lapse in time.

Taking Vacas

Don't be afraid to take breaks to refuel in the middle of the barrage of messages:

- Turn off all distractions by using the "Do Not Disturb" mode when you're working intently, having meetings, or just relaxing.

- Planned Check-Ins: Establish regular intervals for checking your messages to avoid being glued to your phone.

Conscious Communication

Mindful communication is closely linked to effective conversation management:

- Effective Communication: Make sure your statements are succinct and unambiguous to minimize the need for back and forth clarification.

- Empathy: Take the recipient's thoughts and feelings into consideration. Use emojis or, if needed, rephrase to avoid tone misunderstandings.

- Moments Unplugged: Try to set your electronics down and be fully present when you're spending time with your loved ones.

Chapter 4: Exploring the Basics of Apps

This chapter welcomes you to the world of apps, those alluring software programs that transform your iPhone into an endlessly creative toolbox. Apps are the foundation of your device's functionality, offering anything from productivity to entertainment. This chapter will explore the fundamentals of apps, revealing their power and assisting you in finding, setting up, and utilizing them to enhance your online experience.

Application: Digital Environment

The ecosystem on your iPhone is powered by apps. They serve as your entryways to new opportunities, relationships, and services. Every app is a mini-universe with an own set of features and capabilities catered to your need.

Checking out the App Store

Your virtual app store is the App Store. How to Investigate It:

- Tap the App Store icon located on your Home Screen to open the App Store.

- Browse Categories: Look through sections like Games, Productivity, Health & Fitness, and more to find applications that suit your needs.

- Search: To find specific apps by name or phrase, use the search bar.

- App Pages: Open the page for an app by tapping on its icon. You may find reviews, screenshots, information, and more here.

Setting Apps Up

It's like welcoming a new friend into your digital life when you install an app. How to do it is as follows:

- From App Page: Select the "Get" or price button (if the app is paid) on the app page. Use your Apple ID or Touch ID/Face ID to confirm the installation if requested.

- From Search Results: Select the desired app from the list by tapping on it, then proceed with the installation process.

Putting Apps in Order

Your Home Screen resembles a blank canvas that is ready to be filled with your most beloved apps:

- Folders: Drag and drop an app icon onto another to organize related apps into a folder. To improve organization, you can alter the names of your folders.

- Screens and Layouts: To view the various Home Screen pages, swipe left or right. To reorganize or move apps between pages, long-press and drag them.

A Quick Look at Using Apps

This is a sampler of the app store and how you can use it to improve your iPhone experience:

- Social media: Make connections with friends on Twitter, Instagram, and Facebook.

- Productivity: Use apps like Calendar, To-Do Lists, and Notes to increase your productivity.

- Use apps like Candy Crush, Spotify, and YouTube to lose yourself in games, videos, and music for entertainment.

- Stay in touch by using messaging services like Slack, Skype, and WhatsApp.

- Explore practical tools such as the calculator, maps, and weather in Utilities.

Manage and Update Applications

It's critical to update apps because they change over time:

- Updates: A red badge will appear on the App Store icon when updates are available. Select "Update All" or update individual apps after opening the App Store and selecting the "Updates" tab.

- App management: Delete and review apps that you no longer need on a regular basis. To manage the storage of apps, navigate to Settings > General > iPhone Storage.

Boosting Your Online Experience

In the digital realm, apps are your friends that help you with chores, amusement, and exploration. You're accepting the possibility that technology can improve your life as you explore the world of apps. In the upcoming chapters, we'll go more deeply into particular app categories to help you maximize the functionality of your iPhone and turn it into a customized tool for all of your needs.

4.1 Using the App Store

Investigating the App Store

There are numerous methods available in the App Store to find apps that spark your interest:

- Featured: To see the apps that Apple has highlighted, swipe through this section. New releases, popular apps, and carefully chosen collections are frequently among them.

- Browse through a variety of categories, including games, productivity, health and fitness, and more. Every category opens up a universe of apps based on your preferences.

- Look for apps by name, developer, or keyword using the search bar at the top. Once you've typed, tap "Search" to see the results.

Touch Pages: Revealing the Mysteries

Once an app has captured your interest, click on its icon to open its page. This is a veritable gold mine of information:

- App Details: Take a look at this quick summary of the features and advantages of the app.

- Screenshots and Videos: To see the app in action, swipe through the screenshots. Additionally, some apps offer videos for a more engaging preview.

- Look through user reviews and ratings to determine the dependability and quality of the app.

Installing and Downloading Apps

It's time to integrate an intriguing app into your digital life after you find it:

- Tap the "Get" or "Price" button on the app page to download it for free, or the "Price" button to download it for a fee.

- Authenticate: To verify the download, enter your Face ID, Touch ID, or Apple ID password if asked.

Patches and Application Management

Not only can you find new apps on the App Store, but you can also manage your app collection and keep your current apps updated there:

- App updates are available by tapping the "Updates" tab located at the bottom. Select "Update All" to update all of the apps at once, or update each one separately.

- App Management: Tap "Today" at the App Store's bottom, followed by your profile picture, to view your collection of apps. You can manage subscriptions and view the apps you've purchased from this page.

Unlocking Virtual Journeys

Beyond just a storefront for apps, the App Store serves as a portal to innumerable entertainment options, productivity tips, creative tools, and virtual adventures. You're engaging with the pulse of innovation as you browse its virtual aisles and making connections with like-minded users and developers around the world. In the upcoming chapters, we will delve further into particular app categories, giving you the tools to customize your iPhone experience and take advantage of every online opportunity.

4.2 Installing and Deleting Apps

Investigation and Picking:

Explore the App Store to find new apps that suit your needs, interests, or curiosities.

- App Pages: Open the page for an app by tapping on its icon. This page has comprehensive details about the features, reviews, screenshots, and other content related to the app.

Installation

- The Get Button: If the app is free, select the "Get" button from the app page. Click the price button to see if the app is paid.

- Authentication: Use your Face ID, Touch ID, or Apple ID password to authenticate the installation if prompted.

- Wait for the download to finish. A progress indicator will show up next to the app's icon on your home screen. The app is ready for use when the indicator goes away.

Arranging Your Applications: Designing Your Area

Organizing your apps for ease of use and aesthetic appeal can be compared to how an artist arranges colors on a palette:

- Organize your frequently used apps on your primary Home Screen to facilitate effortless access. Drag and drop the icons to where you'd like them to be.

- Folders: Arrange compatible apps into folders. Simply drag the icons of two apps to create a folder; it will do the rest. For clarity, personalize the folder names.

- Extra Screens: To view extra pages from the Home Screen, swipe left. For applications that you want to have easily accessible but are used less often, use these pages.

App Uninstalling:

- Press and hold an app icon on the Home Screen to perform a long press. The app icons will start to jiggle after a short while, and a "X" will show up in the corner.

- Delete: Tap the "X" symbol located on the desired app. You'll receive a confirmation message.

- App icon and data will be erased from your device; confirm deletion by tapping "Delete."

App Deployment:

- Settings: Another option is to offload apps without erasing their data. Navigate to General > iPhone Storage under Settings.

- To offload an app, select it by tapping on it. Offloading saves app data for later use, and you'll have the choice to "Delete App" or "Offload App."

The Skill of Picking

Your digital journey is reflected in the apps you install and keep on your iPhone. While you choose which apps to add to your collection, keep in mind your needs, interests, and available storage. The process of installing and removing apps is a never-ending dance that keeps your device a customized tool for your daily exploits.

In the upcoming chapters, we'll delve deeper into a variety of app categories, giving you the **freedom to investigate, try new things, and interact with the digital world however you see fit. When** you install and remove apps from your iPhone, keep in mind that it's a blank canvas for productivity and creativity, just waiting for you to create your own digital masterpiece.

4.3 Organizing Apps on the Home Screen

Screen at Home on Your Digital Canvas

Consider your Home Screen as an empty space just awaiting your artistic input. A little organizing will turn it into a well-organized masterpiece that expresses your priorities and sense of style.

Setting App Priorities: First Step

The apps that you use the most often are highlighted on the main Home Screen. This is how this stage should be curated:

- Apps you use often, like Messages, Phone, Mail, Calendar, and Notes, should be placed here for easy access.

- Favorites: Think about putting your most preferred contacts in the bottom-of-the-screen dock for easy access.

Folder Creation: The Group of Applications

Similar to musical ensembles, folders are collections of connected apps that play well together. Making a folder:

- Long Press: Tap an app and hold it there until it begins to jiggle.

- To drop an app icon onto another, use the drag and drop method. Both apps will appear inside a folder.

- Customization: To open the folder, tap on it. Drag apps into or out of the folder as necessary. You can edit the folder name by tapping on it.

More Home Screen Pages: Increasing the Symphony

Access more Home Screen pages by swiping left; each page adds a new movement to your symphony. For less often used apps or apps with specialized functions, use these pages:

- Widgets: Think about including widgets with apps that offer quick access to information like the weather, upcoming events on the calendar, or news headlines.

Organizing Apps with Meaning: The Composer's Hand

Think about the logic and flow of your layout when you arrange the apps:

- Classifications: Arrange related applications into folders. For example, apps like Fitness, Meditation, and Health Tracker could be found in a "Health" folder.

- Color Coordination: Use color to arrange apps in a way that makes them visually appealing.

- Symmetry: To achieve a balanced layout, place apps in a symmetrical pattern around the dock or widgets.

Customizing Your Wallcovering: Establishing the Tone

The atmosphere of your Home Screen is influenced by your wallpaper, much like the mood of a performance is set by its backdrop. Select a wallpaper that speaks to you—a picture, a piece of art, or a calm, happy scene.

Your Virtual Proposal

Arranging apps on your Home Screen is akin to creating a digital overture, serving as an introduction to your digital encounters. You're arranging widgets, folders, and apps in a way that maximizes functionality while maintaining style and personalization. We will delve deeply into each of the app categories in the next chapters, allowing you to broaden your digital toolkit and keep crafting your iPhone experience into a masterpiece that speaks to your own rhythm.

Chapter 5: Navigating the Web

Welcome to this chapter, which takes you through the thrilling world of iPhone web browsing—a place where knowledge, amusement, and exploration are all right at your fingertips. Your iPhone serves as a conduit to the vast expanse of the internet in addition to being a communication tool in this digital age. Let's explore the art of web navigation, where webpages transform into uncharted territory.

Safari: Your Web Browser Window

With Safari, you can explore websites, get information, and interact with people around the world online. It's like having your own virtual passport to the internet. To start your web browsing adventure, follow these steps:

- How to use Safari:

- The Safari icon, a blue compass, can be found and tapped on your Home Screen.

- Address Bar: You can enter search terms or website addresses (URLs) in the address bar at the top of the screen.

Getting Around Websites: The Digital Investigation

The internet is your playground once you're in Safari. Here's how to navigate web pages elegantly:

- Type the address of a website into the address bar and press the "Go" key on the keyboard to access that website.

- Bookmarking: To save a webpage for later easy access, tap the share icon (a box with an arrow).

- Tabs: To navigate between different websites without leaving the current page, tap the tabs icon, which is represented by two overlapping squares. This allows you to open multiple tabs.

Scrolling and Zooming: Touch Choreography

Websites resemble dynamic paintings. To explore their content, use natural gestures:

- Pinch to Zoom: On a webpage, pinch your fingers together or apart to zoom in or out.

- Scrolling: Use your finger to swipe up or down to view the content of a webpage.

Reading Mode: Sharp Focus on Clarity

- Website layouts can occasionally be cluttered. You can concentrate on the content by using Safari's Reading mode:

- When available, tap the reader icon (an icon that resembles an open book) in the address bar to switch to reading mode.

Look It Up: The Information Superhighway

Safari serves as an information portal as well. Use it to read articles, find new ideas, and conduct interest-based searches:

- Search Engines: Using the address bar, type your search terms and press "Go" to use the search engine of your choice (usually Google by default).

- With Safari's search suggestions, you can find what you're looking for more quickly as you type.

Security and Privacy: Protecting Your Travels

Safari has built-in safeguards to keep your online privacy and security secure, including:

- Turn on Private Browsing in Safari settings to stop cookies, site data, and browsing history from being saved.

- Installing content blocking applications will allow you to manage the kinds of trackers and content that websites allow.

Holding a Universe of Exploration

Using the web on your iPhone is like setting out on a never-ending adventure. The online world offers a wide range of experiences, from information and news to amusement and interpersonal relationships.

5.1 Browsing with Safari

Tabs: Doors to Parallel Realms

See tabs as entry points that take you to alternate realities, where several websites exist concurrently and are just waiting for you to explore:

- To begin a new browsing journey, tap the tabs icon, which consists of two overlapping squares, located at the bottom of the screen. To explore new horizons, long-press a link to open it in a new tab.

- Tab Management: To move through the tabs you have open, swipe left or right on the tab bar. To end a tab, simply tap the "X" icon, saying "goodbye" to that virtual realm.

Bookmarks: Your Online Reference

Consider bookmarks as your online library, where you store your location within the vast network of the internet:

- To add a bookmark to your digital library, click the share icon, which is a box with an arrow. To store the bookmark, choose a folder, then hit "Save" to add it to the catalog.

- To access your saved bookmarks, tap the bookmarks icon (an open book) at the bottom of the screen. This will take you to your digital library.

Search and Astute Recommendations: Directed Investigation

Use Safari as your guide through the digital maze, offering you helpful suggestions and search functionality.

- Search using the address bar: Type your search terms into the address bar and hit "Go" to start a search using your preferred search engine, most likely Google.

Your Digital Haven for Security and Privacy

With Safari, you can protect your online security and privacy like a fortress:

- To make sure your browsing history, cookies, and site data stay private, turn on Private Browsing in the Safari settings.

- Installing content blocking apps gives you the ability to manage which trackers and content are allowed access to your virtual haven.

Perusing List: Your Individual Archive

Think of your Reading List as your personal gold mine, a carefully chosen selection of articles just waiting for your perusal:

- To save a link in your personal archive, long-press it and choose "Add to Reading List".

- Get to your Reading List by tapping the bookmarks icon and selecting "Reading List," which will provide you access to all of your digital treasures.

5.2 Searching the Internet

The Search Is Underway

The browser on your iPhone can be thought of as the compass that leads you through the vast expanse that is the internet. You can open up a world of information and explore new areas with the help of search engines:

Your Virtual Guides: Search Engines

- Google: By default, Safari searches using Google, which is renowned for providing thorough and quick results.

- Options: Depending on your preferences, you can use the Safari settings to switch to different search engines like Yahoo or Bing.

How to Conduct a Search: The Power of Keywords

- Address Bar Search: Using the keyboard, type keywords directly into the address bar and press "Go" to start a search.

- Search Suggestions: As you type, Safari's intelligent suggestions appear, often anticipating what you're looking for to speed up your search.

Using Search Results to Navigate Your Digital Adventure

Your portal to an endless supply of knowledge is the search results page. How to use it is as follows:

- Links: Use the links to search for websites that are relevant. To access the webpage, tap a link.

- Snippets: Learn what the webpage offers by reading the succinct summaries (snippets) that appear beneath each link.

- Pictures and Videos: Look through the picture and video results to find visual content that relates to your search.

Talking to Your iPhone with Voice Search

- Tap the microphone icon to initiate a voice search from the address bar.

- Natural Language: Talk to your iPhone normally, and it will translate your question into text and run the search.

Chapter 6: Photos and Camera

Welcome to a chapter where Camera and Photos, the colorful brushstrokes of visual storytelling, paint the canvas of your life. In the flick of an eye, your iPhone turns into a magic wand that captures moments, feelings, and memories. We'll delve into the world of photography in this chapter and discover how to capture those fleeting moments and preserve them as priceless keepsakes using the camera on your iPhone.

Watching and Going: A Trip Through Time

- Photos Tab: Go through your images in a chronological order on the "Photos" tab. To view moments in the order they were taken, scroll.

- Years, Months, and Days: Access particular years, months, and even days by using the interactive timeline to relive your experiences.

Revising and Improving: Unleash Your Creative Side

You can edit and perfect your photos in the same way that an artist perfects their creation:

- Edit Button: To access a variety of editing tools, such as enhancing colors or adjusting exposure, open a photo and tap "Edit".

- Use filters to experiment with giving your images different tones and moods.

Making Recordings: Arranging Your Stories

Think of albums as sections in your photographic narrative, a means to arrange and distribute particular photo sets:

- Make albums for events, travels, or themes using the Albums Tab. Navigate to the "Albums" tab to view and control your carefully chosen collections.

- To add photos to an album, select them and then tap the share icon to add them to a new or existing album.

Camera: Your Creative Portal

With the help of the Camera app, you can instantly express your creativity and turn everyday objects into works of art.

Taking Pictures: The Click's Art

Pressing the shutter button will allow you to freeze the moment. Hold down the shutter to take continuous pictures while using the Burst mode.

- Turn on Live Photos to record a little audio and motion along with your pictures.

Capturing Personalities in Portrait Mode

Consider the Portrait mode as a digital brush that expertly blends your subjects into beautifully blurred backgrounds:

- To capture your subject against a dreamy backdrop, select the Portrait mode.

- Lighting Effects: To give your portraits more drama and depth, try out various lighting effects.

Panoramas: Widening Views

Think of panoramas as a single sweep at capturing expansive scenes, a window to breathtaking vistas:

- To capture a panoramic image with sweeping views, choose the Pano mode and adhere to the on-screen guidelines.

Taking in Motion with Time-Lapse and Slo-Mo

Imagine Slo-Mo and Time-Lapse as paintbrushes that allow you to paint time in new dimensions:

- Time-Lapse: Set up your shot and let the camera capture the world changing over time to capture the passage of time.

- Using slow motion, you can capture engrossing videos that highlight minute details that are frequently lost in the rush of daily life.

See the World Through Your Perspective

When you use the Photos and Camera apps on your iPhone, it opens up new creative possibilities. It can be used as a canvas for your photographic narratives as well as a lens to find meaningful moments and moments of beauty. Every album represents a new chapter in your journey, and every click is an artistic endeavor. When you dive into the wonders of photography, never forget that your iPhone is more than just a gadget—it's a time machine, a storyteller, and a creator of lifelong memories.

6.1 Taking Photos and Videos

Taking Pictures: The Verse of Split Seconds

Setting the focus and exposure point is as simple as tapping the screen. Manually adjust the exposure by swiping up or down.

- Burst Mode: Press and hold the shutter button to quickly take a series of pictures one after the other.

- Live Photos: Capture those momentous moments by adding a little bit of sound and movement to your pictures.

Examining Camera Settings: The Creative Toolkit

See the camera modes as a palette of choices, with each mode providing a distinct brushstroke for you to use when creating your visual story:

The Art of Depth in Portrait Mode

To capture subjects in focus against a beautifully blurred background, choose the Portrait mode.

- Lighting Effects: To give your portraits more drama and flair, try out various lighting effects.

Pano Mode: Accepting the Massive

Think of Panorama mode as a doorway to the vast, a means of capturing expansive scenes and vistas that are out of your line of sight:

- Choose Pano mode and adhere to the on-screen instructions to capture the vastness of cityscapes and landscapes.

Painting Time: Time-Lapse

Using Time-Lapse, you can compress hours into seconds by using it as a brush to paint the passage of time:

- Time-Lapse: Arrange your scene and allow the camera to record the scene's changes over time.

Slo-Mo: The Details Dance

Think of slow motion as a dance that reveals hidden details, such as subtleties that would otherwise go unnoticed.

- Create captivating slow-motion videos with Slo-Mo to transform everyday activities into captivating sequences.

Video Recording: Storytelling in Motion

Think of videos as dynamic narratives that tell stories in motion:

- Flip to Video: To transition to Video mode, swipe the camera's mode selector.

Multiple Views from the Front and Rear Cameras

As two distinct lenses, your front and rear cameras will each provide a different perspective.

- Tap the camera flip icon to quickly flip between the front and rear cameras.

- Selfies: To capture your expressions and emotions, take selfies and make video calls using the front camera.

6.2 Viewing and Editing Photos

The Memorable Images Gallery

Think of your Photos app as a gallery, showcasing the works of art in your life—a selection of images that each tell a different chapter in your story.

Observing and Orienting: A Trip Along Memory Lane

- Photos Tab: Explore your visual timeline and relive every moment as it was captured by clicking on the "Photos" tab.

- Years, Months, and Days: Explore particular years, months, and days using the interactive timeline to relive your memories.

Making Albums: Arranging Your Graphic Chapters

View albums as sections of your visual autobiography, a means of compiling and distributing particular moments and ideas:

- Create records for occasions, travels, or emotions under the Albums Tab. The "Albums" tab allows you to view and manage your carefully chosen collections.

- To add photos to an album, select the images and then select the share icon to add them to a new or existing album.

Revision and Improvement: Crafting Your Graphic Story

You can edit your images to bring out their genuine essence, much like a sculptor does with their marble masterpiece:

- Edit Button: To access a variety of tools, such as exposure adjustment and color correction, open a photo and select "Edit".

- Play around with filters to give your images a variety of tones and moods.

- Cropping and Adjusting: Organizing Your Viewpoint

- Think of cropping and straightening as the framing of your viewpoint, a method to highlight the most important aspects of a picture:

- Crop Tool: When in Edit mode, use the crop tool to eliminate distractions and draw attention to your main topic.

- Straighten: For a more professional composition, align the lines in your image or adjust the horizon.

Portrait Lighting: Artfully Creating the Effect of Light

Consider Portrait Lighting as a tool to shape the illumination of your subjects, a digital lighting studio:

- Select from a variety of lighting effects after entering portrait mode to give your portraits more depth and drama.

Your Creative Safety Net: How to Undo and Revert

Consider the undo and revert function as your creative safety net, allowing you to experiment with edits without fear:

- Undo: To undo recent changes and restore your iPhone to its original state, shake it.

- Revert: When in Edit mode, select "Revert" to remove all edits and return the image to its initial state.

Tell and Treasure: Narratives Exchanged

See sharing as a means of giving away your memories, a means of fostering happiness and fostering connections via your visual stories:

- Share Button: You can share photos via social media, email, messages, and more by tapping the share icon.

- Create shared albums with friends and family so you can work together on preserving memories.

6.3 Sharing Memories with Others

Greetings from a chapter that explores the enchantment of bonding through sharing memories with others. Learn how to share the laughs, stories, and feelings that are captured in your images and videos by using your iPhone as a bridge. You will learn about the art of bringing happiness, strengthening relationships, and weaving a virtual tapestry of shared experiences in this chapter.

Exchange of Images and Videos: Moments Enhanced

- Press the "Share" button to reveal a plethora of options for sharing your images and videos.

- Messages: Use messaging to send your recollections straight to your loved ones.

- Social Media: Share your images and videos on social media sites to reach a larger audience.

AirDrop: Instant Happiness

Consider AirDrop to be a kind of teleporter for memories—a smooth method of exchanging media with Apple devices in the vicinity:

- AirDrop Button: From the AirDrop list, select the recipient's device by tapping the share icon.

- Acceptance: Upon notification, the recipient has the option to accept the content right away.

Combined Stories: Joint Albums

Think of shared albums as an online family get-together where everyone shares their pictures and stories:

- To establish a shared album, select the "+" icon located in the Albums tab. Ask your loved ones to help as well.

- Content Addition: Each participant may contribute their own images and videos to the collection.

Collaborative Editing: Optimal Co-Creation

Think of cooperative editing as a way to enhance memories through artistic collaboration:

- Edit Shared Album: Participants can alter images in the shared album to collectively enhance the memories.

Reliving the Past through Memory Sharing

Think of memory sharing as a way to revisit bygone times with friends and family, like a time capsule:

- Discover carefully chosen memories to share by browsing the "For You" tab.

- To share a carefully selected collection of memories with friends and family, simply tap the share icon on a memory card.

Sharing Slideshows: Online Narration

Slideshow sharing can be thought of as a digital theater that allows you to display your images and videos in an eye-catching order:

- Share Icon: To produce a dynamic visual presentation, tap the share icon and choose "Play Slideshow".

Adding Vibrance to Messages with Live Photos and Videos

Consider Live Photos and Videos as living messages—a means of communicating feelings in addition to images:

- Messages: To liven up your conversations, send live photos and videos through your messages.

Chapter 7: Entertainment and Media

Greetings from a chapter that leads to a world of creativity, inspiration, and immersion: media and entertainment. With movies, music, books, and more at your fingertips, your iPhone becomes a portal. You'll explore the wide world of entertainment in this chapter, learning how your gadget can function as a movie theater, library, and symphony all in one.

The Amusement Haven

Consider your iPhone to be a treasure chest full of entertainment that can transport you from the ordinary into worlds of discovery, feeling, and amazement.

Television Series and Films: Your Own Home Theater

Movies and TV series can be accessed by opening the Apple TV app.

- Rent or Buy: Easily peruse and purchase movies and series from the app.

- Streaming Services: Look into well-known streaming services that provide a range of streaming content.

Literature and Books: Your Virtual Library

Think of your iPhone as a library—a storehouse of knowledge, creativity, and stories:

- Apple Books: Check out a variety of books, including both new and classic titles, by opening Apple Books.

- Audiobooks: Whether traveling, working out, or just unwinding, listen to audiobooks.

Playing games: Your Fun Playground

Consider your iPhone to be a gaming console, a place where you can play games and take on challenges online:

- Play games on the App Store: From light puzzles to deep role-playing games, there are a ton of games available.

- Play games with other players from around the world to establish connections with friends.

Your Information Hub for News and Magazines

Imagine your iPhone as a newsstand, a central source of information that provides you with the latest news and events:

- News App: Read news stories from a range of sources to stay up to date.

- Magazines: Examine online editions of periodicals addressing a range of fascinating subjects.

The blending of reality between augmented and virtual reality

You can immerse yourself in virtual and augmented reality by using your iPhone as a window into alternate dimensions.

- Games and Apps: Find games and apps that make use of AR and VR technology to create interactive experiences.

Discovering Novel Worlds

You're entering new worlds, discovering fresh viewpoints, and broadening your horizons with each tap, swipe, and interaction—you're not just consuming entertainment. As you traverse the worlds of media and entertainment, never forget that your gadget is a portal to happy, contemplative, and intimate moments rather than just a tool. It serves as a canvas for you to paint your feelings on, a stage for you to act out stories, and a conduit for the wonders of human imagination.

7.1 Listening to Music and Podcasts

The Harmony Right at Your Fingertips

Consider your iPhone to be a miniature orchestra in your pocket, full of tunes, beats, and narratives just waiting to be explored.

- Your Sonic Oasis is Apple Music.

- Listen to a huge selection of songs, albums, and playlists by opening Apple Music.

- Explore and Find: Make use of the search function to track down particular songs, musicians, or genres. Depending on your tastes, find new music.

- Curated Playlists: Listen to carefully selected playlists for a variety of times and moods, including energizing workouts and calm afternoons.

Making Playlists: Sculpting Your Sound Story

Think of making playlists as a kind of narrative weaving—song selections that encapsulate your feelings and experiences:

- New Playlist: Click "New Playlist" to begin creating your own unique musical experience.

- Search for songs to add to your playlist or browse your library to add them.

Turn it Up and Back Down: Customizing Your Journey

Consider using shuffle and repeat as tools to customize your experience, so you may go through your collection or go back and revisit your favorites:

- Shuffle: Press the shuffle icon to listen to music in an arbitrary sequence.

- Repeat: To loop a playlist or song, tap the repeat icon.

Podcast Listening: Increasing Your Mind

Podcasts can be seen of as a global conversation that offers you the chance to learn, laugh, and get fresh insights.

- Open Apple Podcasts to discover a wide selection of podcasts covering a range of subjects.

- Explore and Search: To locate podcasts that pique your interest, peruse the categories or utilize the search function.

Improving the Experience of Listening

You may customize your listening experience on your iPhone by thinking of it as an amplifier for your emotions:

- Equalizer Settings: To fine-tune the sound according to your audio preferences, use the equalizer settings in the Settings app.

- Establish a volume restriction to safeguard your hearing and to guarantee safe listening levels.

Memories and Music Go Together Perfectly

You are more than just a listener with every note and word—you are a time traveler, an evaluator of feelings, and a seeker of knowledge. Your life is a tale, and every song you listen to or podcast episode you watch becomes a bookmark. Remember that your iPhone is more than just a gadget when you start enjoying music and podcasts; it's a medium for connecting with artists, finding inspiration, and discovering the symphony of human creativity. It can accompany you on your travels, offer comfort, and serve as a window into the seemingly endless worlds of stories and music.

7.2 Watching Videos and Movies

Your Portable Theater

Think of your iPhone as a magical lantern that can transport imaginary and emotional realms onto its lit screen.

- The Entertainment Hub App for Apple TV

- Explore a wide range of films, TV series, and other content by opening the Apple TV app.

- Explore content that has been highlighted and suggestions that have been made based on your personal tastes.

Renting vs Purchasing: The Magic of On-Demand Films

Consider purchasing and renting films as bringing forth cinematic experiences whenever it suits you:

- Movie Details: Press on a film to see synopsis, trailers, and additional material.

- Choose "Rent" or "Buy" to get the movie and watch it on your device.

Various Options for Streaming Services

Think of streaming services as doors leading to other content universes, where you can discover a wide selection of films and TV series to watch:

- Subscription Services: Use their specific applications to access well-known streaming services.

- Content can be filtered by genres, themes, and suggested readings.

Modifying Replay: Customizing the Experience

Think of playback options as a way to personalize and adjust your watching experience:

- Audio and Subtitles: Modify the audio language and subtitle options to improve comprehension and enjoyment.

- Playback Pace: Adjust the playback speed to suit your own pace.

Putting Together Your Watchlist: Selecting What to Watch

Think of building a watchlist as a personal library of stuff to peruse, similar to collecting tickets for future adventures:

- To add movies and TV series to your watchlist for convenient access at a later time, simply tap the "Add" icon.

- To access your curated watchlist, navigate to the "Library" section.

Enjoyment Anywhere with Offline Viewing

To enjoy movies and shows offline without an internet connection, picture yourself carrying about a portable theater:

- To store content for viewing at a later time, look for the download symbol.

- To access downloaded content, navigate to the "Downloaded" tab under the "Library" section.

7.3 Reading Books and News

Apple Books: A Haven for Books

- Explore Genres: Click Apple Books to access an extensive library of books on a wide range of topics and genres.

- Check out a few books before you buy them, then pick the ones that really grab your attention.

- Customize Reading: For a comfortable reading experience, change the backdrop color, text size, and lighting.

Reading Modes: Matching Your Reading Style

To have the best possible reading experience, think of reading modes as lenses that may be adjusted to your preferences:

- Day and Night Mode: Slide to the dark mode to read comfortably in dimly lit areas.

- Choose a reading style that works for you by either scrolling or turning pages.

Audiobooks: Hearing Stories Spoken Aloud

Consider audiobooks as a method to read while multitasking—imagine stories whispering in your ears:

- Choose from a vast array of audiobooks on a variety of topics by exploring the selection.

- Playback speed should be adjusted to correspond with your listening speed.

News App: Your One-stop Shop for News

Consider the News app as a window to the outside world, a platform that informs you about current issues and world happenings:

- Investigate News: Launch the News app to view articles from various publishers.

- Get customized news recommendations based on your interests with the help of the personalized feed.

Chapter 8: Accessibility Features

Greetings and welcome to the Accessibility Features chapter, which highlights the power of technology for inclusivity. Imagine your iPhone as a beacon of accessibility. Explore a plethora of features that make it possible for everyone, with or without disabilities, to interact, navigate, and enjoy the digital world with ease.

VoiceOver: Encouraging Words

Consider VoiceOver as your virtual assistant—a narrator that speaks descriptions to you while you navigate your device:

- Activation: Open Accessibility > VoiceOver > Turn it on.

- Touch navigation is available, along with VoiceOver's voice descriptions of screen elements.

Magnifier: Enlarging the Global Image

Consider Magnifier as a digital magnifying glass, a tool that helps you focus on details:

- To activate Magnifier, turn it on under the accessibility options.

- Use: You can enlarge text, objects, and scenes in real time by using your camera.

Easy on the Eyes: Intelligent Reversing and Dim Mode

Consider Smart Invert and Dark Mode as calming modes that will improve readability and lessen glare in your eyes:

- Smart Invert: Flip your display's colors to make it easier on your eyes in dimly lit areas.

- Turn on a dark theme to improve reading comprehension and lessen eye strain.

Accessible Content with Closed Captions and Subtitles

Consider subtitles and closed captions as understanding bridges that let you interact with video content:

- Activation: In compatible apps, turn on closed captions or subtitles.

- Personalization: Adjust the language and look of the captions.

Personalized Touch with AssistiveTouch

Consider AssistiveTouch as your personal touch assistant that allows you to use gestures to communicate with your device:

- To activate AssistiveTouch, turn it on in the accessibility settings.

- Create personalized gestures and shortcuts to make things easier to use.

Quick Access is an accessibility shortcut.

To swiftly access crucial accessibility functions, think of the Accessibility Shortcut as your secret key:

- To activate the accessibility shortcut, configure it in the accessibility settings.

- Triple-Press: To enable your selected accessibility features, triple-press the side or home buttons.

An Experience That Empowers Everyone

You're embracing the potential of technology to foster a more welcoming and encouraging environment with each activation and adjustment—you're not just changing the settings. Your iPhone turns into a powerful instrument, a link to self-sufficiency, and a platform for showcasing each person's own talents. Remember that your gadget is a travel companion—one that will help create a digital environment that is more varied, inclusive, and compassionate—as you explore the world of accessibility features.

8.1 Enabling Accessibility Settings

Increasing Visibility with Display and Text Size

Think of the Display & Text Size options as an aesthetic tailor who may change aspects to suit your preferences:

- font Size: Modify the font size to make it easier to read.

- Bold Text: To improve legibility and contrast, make text bold.

VoiceOver: A Story Told in Voice

Consider the VoiceOver settings as a narrator guiding you through the capabilities on your device, acting as its storyteller:

- VoiceOver Gestures: Use your device's touch and audible feedback to navigate with VoiceOver gestures.

- Rotor Settings: Tailor the VoiceOver rotor to your preferences for easier navigation.

A Hint of Convenience with AssistiveTouch

Consider the AssistiveTouch settings as your helper, a method to make device interactions easier:

- Custom Motions: Design unique motions to carry out particular tasks.

- Customize Home Button: You can choose how AssistiveTouch responds to the buttons on your device.

Flip Colors: Distinct Viewpoints

Consider the Invert Colors options as a tool to alter the appearance of your device, a gateway to alternate worlds:

- Smart Invert: Reverse colors with Smart Invert to ease eye strain.

- Use the standard invert function to flip all of the colors on your device.

8.2 Using VoiceOver and Zoom

Your Entryway to Broad-Based Communication. Think of your iPhone as a talking, magnifying friend that gives you the confidence and ease to navigate around the gadget.

VoiceOver Personalization: Crafting a Unique Experience

View the VoiceOver settings as a set of sculpting tools that let you customize the way you interact with the system:

- Speech Rate: You can change VoiceOver's speaking pace to whatever suits you best.

- Pitch and Volume: Tailor VoiceOver speech to your preferred pitch and volume.

Zoom: The Digital Magnification Len

Zoom is a tool that magnifies content to make details more obvious and interactions more accurate. Think of it as your magnifying glass:

- To activate Zoom, first go to "Accessibility" in the "Settings" app.

- Learn how to zoom in and out using gestures by double-tapping with three fingers, for example.

Zoom Customization: Fitting Your Requirements

Think of Zoom settings as a tape measure used by tailors to make sure everything fits perfectly:

- Zoom Region: Select between a windowed zoom area or full screen zoom.

- Maximum Zoom Level: Choose the greatest magnification that pleases you.

8.3 Customizing Text and Display

Your Unique Style on Show

See your iPhone as a gallery, where you may arrange images to complement your experience and speak to you.

Mode of View: Tailoring Color Look

View Mode settings are similar to filters on a camera lens, allowing you to customize the display colors to your taste:

- Color Filters: A variety of color filters are available to meet various visual requirements.

- Color Tint: To change the display's temperature, adjust the color tint.

Automatic Brightness and Night Mode: Calm Lighting

Consider Auto-Brightness and Night Shift settings as your go-to sources for lighting design that is easy on the eyes:

- Use the auto-brightness feature to let your smartphone change the screen's brightness in response to outside lighting.

- Turn on Night Shift to improve your quality of sleep by limiting your exposure to blue light in the evening.

Dark Mode: Beautiful Beauty

Consider the Dark Mode options as if they were an artist's sketchbook, giving your interface a clean, dark aesthetic:

- Appearance: Select between Light and Dark Modes, or set the latter to run only during certain hours.

- App-Specific Settings: Some apps allow for the customisation of separate dark mode settings.

Your Visual Identity with Wallpaper and Screensaver

Consider the wallpaper and screensaver options as brushstrokes on a canvas to customize the appearance of your device:

- Wallpaper: You can select one of the pre-installed wallpapers or upload your own.

- Screensaver: Customize the lock screen experience by adjusting the screensaver settings.

Opening Up Your Visual World

You're creating an interface that's specifically suited to your eyes, your tastes, and your style with each modification and change, not merely changing it. Your iPhone starts to symbolize your visual comfort and an extension of who you are. Remember that your device is more than just a screen when you delve into the realm of text and display customization; it's a mirror reflecting your style, a canvas that fits your wants, and evidence that technology can be tailored to your specific visual requirements.

Chapter 9: Tips for Better Usage

Your Path to Mastery

Consider your iPhone a toolkit: an assortment of devices that, when used intelligently, may improve your productivity, inventiveness, and security.

Tips for Navigating: Getting Around Like a Pro

Think of navigational tactics as graceful routes that lead you and enable you to get at your destination quickly:

- App Switcher: On iPhones with Face ID, swipe up from the bottom to open the app switcher. On iPhones without Face ID, double-tap the home button to switch between previously used applications.

Shortcuts: Increasing Task Speed

Think of shortcuts as magic teleportations that allow you to complete activities quickly and easily with a single tap or gesture:

- Control Center Shortcuts: You may personalize the Control Center by adding shortcuts to commonly used menu items and features.

Notification Management: Remaining Up to Date

To ensure that crucial updates are not overlooked, think of notification management as a neat desk:

- Notification grouping: Arrange alerts according to apps to simplify your notification area.

- Notification Settings: To change the way that apps alert you, navigate to "Settings" > "Notifications".

Optimizing Battery Life: Extending Power

Consider optimizing battery life as a conservationist strategy that stores energy for times when you most need it:

- How Your Battery Is Used: Go to "Settings" > "Battery" to get usage statistics for your battery.

- Low Power Mode: When your battery is almost empty, switch on Low Power Mode to preserve it.

Best Practices for Security: Protecting Your Device

Consider security procedures as a fortification that guards your information and privacy against online dangers:

- Turn on biometric authentication (Face ID/Touch ID) for increased security.

- Two-Factor Authentication: For an additional degree of security, enable two-factor authentication for your Apple ID.

9.1 Extending Battery Life

Batteries Insights: Lighting Usage

Battery insights can be thought of as a torch that illuminates the energy use of your device:

- Battery Usage: Select "Settings" > "Battery" to view the apps that use the most battery life.

- Battery Health: To guarantee optimum performance, explore the "Battery" settings to check the condition of your battery.

Managing Updates with a Background App Refresh

Think of the background app refresh as a flow valve that controls which apps are permitted to update in the background:

- App Refresh Settings: Go to "Settings" > "General" > "Background App Refresh" to turn off updates for applications that don't need to sync all the time.

Location Services: Skillfully Navigating

Consider location services as an energy-saving feature for some apps, and as a GPS tracker for others.

- Location Services: Utilize "Settings" > "Privacy" > "Location Services" to control which applications have access to your location.

- App-specific Location: Using the "While Using" or "Never" options, configure the location for each particular app.

Email Push: Strategic Syncing

Consider push email as a method of delivering mail; you may decide how and when your device retrieves fresh messages:

- Fetch New Data: You may change how often your device looks for new emails by going to "Settings" > "Mail" > "Accounts" > "Fetch New Data".

- Fetch Schedule: To save more battery life, extend the fetch interval or opt for manual fetching.

Organizing Background Activity: Setting Task Priorities

Think of controlling background activity as a to-do list where more critical chores are prioritized above less urgent ones:

- App Notifications: To cut down on background activities, disable notifications for any unimportant apps.

- To control which apps can refresh in the background, navigate to "Settings" > "General" > "Background App Refresh".

9.2 Securing Your iPhone

Your Personal Privacy Guard

Consider your iPhone to be a fortress, a safe haven that protects your experiences and private data from prying eyes and online criminals.

Including Further Layers in Two-Factor Authentication

Consider two-factor authentication to be similar to a double-lock system, where access to your digital domain requires several keys:

- To activate your Apple ID, go to "Settings" > [your name] > "Password & Security" and enable two-factor authentication.

Getting Around Permissions for Apps

Think of app permissions as guardians, allowing access to only those apps that are actually necessary:

- Location, camera, microphone, and other app permissions can be managed by going to "Settings" > "Privacy".

- Background App Refresh: To manage data sharing, restrict which apps have the ability to refresh in the background.

Find My: Monitoring and Recuperation

Consider Find My Settings as a search party, allowing you to locate and locate your device in the event that it is lost:

- Activation: To enable "Find My iPhone," navigate to "Settings" > [your name] > "Find My."

- Lost Mode: Turn on Lost Mode to see contact details and remotely lock your smartphone.

Software Updates: Increasing Security

Consider software updates as fortifying your device and preventing it from being vulnerable to known exploits:

- Upgrade the software on your device to the most recent version by going to "Settings" > "General" > "Software Update."

Security Consciousness: The Greatest Defense

Think of security awareness as your on-duty watchdog, keeping you informed and ready to respond to any threats:

- Phishing Awareness: Exercise caution while responding to shady emails, messages, or websites that request personal data.

Chapter 10: Personalizing Your iPhone

This chapter, "Personalizing Your iPhone," enables you to use your creative abilities. You'll go on a creative adventure using your iPhone as a canvas, turning it into a reflection of your tastes, identity, and sense of style. You will learn how to create an interface that both expresses your aesthetic and your digital self in this chapter.

Your Voice, Your iPhone

Consider your iPhone to be a blank canvas, a way to highlight your individuality, hobbies, and personality.

Backgrounds: Creating an Ambience

Consider wallpapers as digital paintbrushes that apply strokes to your gadget, enhancing its color and aesthetic appeal.

- Built-in Wallpapers: Your iPhone comes pre-installed with a selection of both dynamic and still wallpapers.

- Custom Wallpapers: To add something really unique, use your own photos as the background.

Widgets and App Icons: Aesthetic Coherence

Consider widgets and app icons to be your creative palette, and arrange them to produce a visual harmony:

- App Icons: Using photos that complement your preferred style and shortcuts, create unique app icons.

- Widgets: Arrange widgets so that they quickly highlight information that is important to you on your home screen.

Personalized Commands for Siri Shortcuts

Consider Siri Shortcuts to be your personal assistant, generating shortcuts for routine tasks you complete:

- To create personalized voice commands and automate chores, use the Shortcuts app.

- Custom Icon and Phrase: Add a personal touch to your shortcuts by adding custom icons and phrases.

Dynamic App Store: Well-Ordered Exploration

See the App Library as your personal digital library, one that automatically arranges apps and facilitates easy app discovery:

- To access the App Library, either swipe to the right of the home screen page or pull down from the home screen.

- Apps may be quickly found by utilizing the search bar and suggested app categories.

Gatekeepers of Access: App Permissions

Think of app permissions as gatekeepers, permitting only authorized individuals to access your sensitive data:

- Manage when and how applications can access your location information with Location Services.

- Camera and Microphone: Only allow access to the camera and microphone for apps that actually require it.

Protecting Your Identity with Encryption

Consider data protection settings as your safe, keeping confidential information safe and encrypted:

- Turn on biometric authentication and passcodes for security purposes to safeguard your device.

- Data Encryption: All of the information on your iPhone is encrypted, so that only people with permission can access it.

Limiting Tracking on Websites and Apps

See the privacy settings on websites and apps as curtains that block out unwanted data collection from your interactions.

- To control how websites track your behavior, navigate to "Settings" > "Safari" in Safari.

- Get an App Privacy Report to gain more control over how applications utilize your data.

Notification Center: Setting Up the Group

See your alerts as performers gathered on a large stage, which is the Notification Center.

- The Notification Center can be accessed by swiping down from the top of the screen.

- Notification Grouping: Organize the center by grouping notifications according to apps.

Styles of Notification: Creating the Melody

Consider alert types as notes in a musical composition, each adding to the overall harmony of your digital experience:

- Banner Notifications: Select a banner style to display brief, subdued notifications at the top of the screen.

- Alert Notifications: For clear, interactive alerts that demand action, select the alert style.

Bonus: Glossary of Terms

In this chapter, you'll uncover a collection of definitions, demystifying the language of technology.

iOS:

The operating system that runs on iPhones, iPads, and iPod Touch devices.

3G/4G/5G:

Generations of mobile network technology that provide internet and data communication. The higher the number, the more advanced and faster the technology.

AirDrop:

A feature that allows for the wireless transfer of files between Apple devices.

Airplane Mode:

A setting that disables all wireless communications (Wi-Fi, cellular data, Bluetooth).

App Store:

Apple's online marketplace where you can download applications ("apps") for your iPhone.

Apple ID:

A personal account used to access Apple services, such as the App

Store, iCloud, and iMessage.

Backup:

A copy of your iPhone's data that can be used to restore information if your device is lost, stolen, or not working properly.

Bluetooth:

A wireless technology used for short-range connections between devices.

Control Center:

A feature accessed by swiping down from the upper right corner of the iPhone's screen, which allows quick access to various settings and functions.

Do Not Disturb:

A setting that silences calls, alerts, and notifications on your iPhone for a period you specify.

Face ID:

A facial recognition technology used to unlock the iPhone and authenticate transactions.

Find My iPhone:

A feature that allows you to locate, lock, or erase your iPhone if it's lost or stolen.

iCloud:

Apple's online storage service that lets you store data such as photos, contacts, and backups, and sync them across your Apple devices.

iMessage:

Apple's messaging service that allows you to send text, photos, videos, and more to other Apple devices.

iTunes:

Apple's software used to buy, organize, and play digital music and videos. Also used for backups and restoring iPhone data.

Jailbreak:

A modification that removes restrictions on the iPhone's operating system, allowing for greater customization but also increased security risks.

Location Services:

Features that use your geographical location to improve the functionality of certain apps.

Memoji:

Customized animated avatars that can be used in Messages and FaceTime.

Notification Center:

The area where all your alerts, messages, and updates are displayed. Accessed by swiping down from the top of the screen.

Portrait Mode:

A feature in the Camera app that blurs the background to make the subject stand out.

Safari:

Apple's web browser.

Siri:

Apple's voice-activated assistant that can perform tasks and answer questions for you.

Touch ID:

A fingerprint recognition feature to unlock the iPhone and authenticate transactions.

Two-Factor Authentication:

An extra layer of security for your Apple ID that requires not only a password but also verification from another device.

Wi-Fi:

A wireless networking technology that allows your iPhone to connect to the Internet.

Animoji:

Animated emoji characters that mimic your facial expressions, used in Messages and FaceTime.

Apple Pay:

Apple's mobile payment and digital wallet service that lets you make payments using the iPhone, Apple Watch, or iPad.

Apple Watch:

A smartwatch developed by Apple that can be paired with an iPhone for added functionality like fitness tracking and notifications.

Autocorrect:

A text input feature that automatically corrects typing errors.

Dark Mode:

A feature that changes the appearance of the interface elements to darker colors, often easier on the eyes in low-light conditions.

Family Sharing:

A feature that allows up to six family members to share App Store purchases, Apple subscriptions, and an iCloud storage plan.

Force Touch:

A pressure-sensitive touch technology on some older iPhone models that triggers additional options in certain apps and settings.

Handoff:

A feature that allows tasks to be continued across Apple devices, such as starting an email on an iPhone and finishing it on a Mac.

Home Screen:

The main display screen that houses app icons and widgets, accessed upon unlocking the device.

Live Photos:

A feature that records what happens 1.5 seconds before and after a still photo is taken, resulting in a photo that comes to life when touched.

Low Power Mode:

A setting that minimizes battery usage when the iPhone's battery level drops below a certain percentage.

Night Shift:

A feature that adjusts the colors of your display to the warmer end of the spectrum during the evening to help you sleep better.

QuickType:

Apple's predictive text feature that suggests words as you type.

Screen Time:

A feature that tracks how much time you spend on your device and helps you set limits for app usage.

Widgets:

Small applications that provide quick access to frequently used data and functions, like weather, calendar, and news, directly from the Home Screen.

Conclusion

As we wrap up this guide, it's evident that the iPhone is more than just a gadget; it's a versatile tool designed to simplify and enrich various aspects of our daily lives. From its intuitive interface to its myriad capabilities, the iPhone truly offers a holistic user experience.

In this book, we delved into a wide range of topics that every iPhone user should be familiar with. Starting with the fundamentals of the device's interface in Chapter 1, we moved through the essential procedures for setting up your iPhone, making and receiving calls, and even managing your contacts in Chapter 2.

Understanding the iPhone's communication features was the focus of Chapter 3, where we examined everything from simple text messages to the more sophisticated iMessage system. With the foundational knowledge in place, we then explored the ecosystem of apps that make the iPhone a true powerhouse, as discussed in Chapter 4.

Towards the end, we equipped you with essential tips for extending your battery life, securing your device, and personalizing it to suit your unique needs and tastes. Whether you're a novice iPhone user or someone looking to explore the full range of capabilities your device has to offer, we hope this guide has been valuable.

It's incredible how a single device can serve as a phone, a camera, an entertainment center, and much more. This guide aimed to make mastering your iPhone an enjoyable and rewarding journey. Now that you're well-versed in your iPhone's functionalities, it's time to make the most out of this extraordinary device.

Thank you for choosing "iPhone for Seniors" as your go-to resource for everything iPhone. We wish you endless discoveries and joy as you continue to explore what your iPhone has to offer

Made in the USA
Las Vegas, NV
15 December 2023

82942420R00049